Janey Mac goes to Nauru

Also by Janey Mac and published by Ginninderra Press
Jany Mac Goes to War

Janey Mac

Janey Mac goes to Nauru

Janey Mac goes to Nauru
ISBN 978 1 76041 596 9
Copyright © Janey Mac 2018
Cover design and photography by Janey Mac
Music tablature devised by Janey Mac

First published 2018 by
Ginninderra Press
PO Box 3461 Port Adelaide 5015
www.ginninderrapress.com.au

Contents

Introduction	7
…and a new road: How to get to Nauru #1	17
Coming in to Pleasant Island: How to get to Nauru #2	18
Nauru, First Impressions	19
Naurumour #1	20
Locals	26
Nauru Refugee Blues #1	27
Horse trading with the US	28
In the Heart of Darkness	29
Naurumour #2	30
Any Hamid or Muhammed or	34
Recreation	35
Asylum seekers on Nauru	36
It didn't happen that way	38
The room	40
A senseless place to be	45
Wild dogs on Nauru	46
How to get to Nauru #3	47
Two beers	56
In Protest	59
Naurumour #3	60
Mehdi's song	62
Three scenes	65
How to get to Nauru #4	68
Nauru Refugee Blues #2	74
The evening before I fly out	76
Amicus Nick Martin *sed magis amica veritas*	77
The final few	79
Resignation Letter	81
Email from a refugee granted a visa to the States	84

Introduction

Like most people, I enjoy a quiet life, eventful in its own limited way, but…well, quiet in the absence of major upheavals, in the absence of trauma. Like most people. And, like most people, I'm reasonably content to go to work on a more or less daily basis and to write during my non-leisure, leisure time. And again, like most people, I'm open to change as long as it's limited to the kind of change that doesn't really intrude on my quiet life.

So when I saw the position on Seek.com.au for someone like me to work on Nauru for a finite contract period, I thought, *why not?* After all, it would be a change in location only and, although I'd read plenty about Nauru, like most people, I had little idea of where it was or what it was like. Really like.

So I applied for, and got, the job. And flew out from Brisbane at 07.00 on a hot Thursday morning in late December 2016. I had no expectations because I knew so little, but I found the idea of working with what I imagined to be pretty disadvantaged people an attractive one: I'd been working with a diverse cohort of nationalities in the education field, most of whom were also relatively disadvantaged, for a couple of years, so this would probably be more of the same, but in an exotic locale.

My naiveté was astounding, especially in the face of my normal cynicism.

I have never seen such a brutalised and beaten bunch of people. The asylum seekers and refugees looked ragged in spirit, if not necessarily in appearance. They were, on the surface, ingratiating and often obsequious, though I felt that, beneath the surface, they were angry and resentful. Not all of them, obviously, but the overall feel certainly supported an 'us and them' attitude. Did they have cause for such an attitude? In a very short time of being on the island, I saw that the majority of expat workers cared a great deal about the asylum seekers and refugees, and I saw that the majority of expats quite often ignored policy in favour of humanity. So, why the resentment? Why the anger?

One of the first refugees I had a conversation with was a twenty-four-year-old apprentice baker. Mohammed had been in refugee camps for twenty-two years, he said, first in Bangladesh, then in Malaysia and now in Nauru. He knew nothing else and he was a smiley, attractive young guy. He told me that, not long before we met, he'd saved enough money from his AU$4 an hour job to buy a small motorbike (a 90cc moped, ubiquitous on the island). Within two hours of having bought it, he said, a group of local youth had knocked him off it, beaten him up and stolen the bike. He reported the incident to the police but nothing happened. Mohammed was saving up for another bike.

In the same room, at the time I was hearing this story, an Iranian foursome – two married couples in their late thirties and early forties – were talking among themselves. I approached and introduced myself and tried to make general (inept under the circumstances) conversation. Very soon, I was hearing about how they'd been fishing together a couple of weeks earlier. A group of locals, young and drunk, attacked them and stole their fishing equipment, rudimentary as it was. Did they go to the police? What was the point?

I started to understand the anger and resentment. But that was only the beginning. The instances of physical abuse, threats, intimidation and theft were legion. In not a single case that I heard about did the police take action if the perpetrators were local. In addition to which, several asylum seekers and refugees had reported attacks to the Australian Border Force, the widely feared uber-police on the island. The ABF showed no interest whatsoever: these, they said, were local police matters.

Among the expat workers, those working for the service provider company, there were a good number who were liked and trusted by the asylum seekers and refugees and I quickly established myself as one of them. In this way, I reckoned I'd become privy to stories that I could collate into an information volume: poetry, essays and short stories. I had done this before in *Janey Mac Goes to War* and it was a format that

I enjoyed and that I thought would suit the environment well, as it would provide irony and bathos as well as, I hoped, poignancy.

But before I started, I knew I'd have to learn the history of Nauru in the refugee picture, and I'd have to learn why Australia thought to involve such a small player in such a potentially big scenario.

Why Nauru?

When the Mossack Fonseca law firm's 200,000+ documents were leaked to the German press in 2015, they caused seismic tremors throughout the financial world. The Panama company had offered confidential legal services as well as corporate service provisions across the global financial spectrum to individual, commercial and national entities, and the suddenly-made-public information shed a blinding light on an array of activities that many would have preferred remained hidden in perpetuity. One of the main problems highlighted in the released information was that, while offshore wealth protection may well be a hundred per cent legal, fraud, tax evasion and money laundering are not. And there was evidence of a plethora of fraud, tax evasion and money laundering, despite the OECD having issued strict guidelines for international banking cooperation in an attempt to curtail such activities among others. These guidelines included a system of information exchange between banking regulators on request; a signed multilateral agreement on information standards by member states; and a commitment to a fully automated information exchange in either 2017 or 2018.

Three countries failed to comply with all of the guidelines: Panama, Lebanon and Vanuatu. These were expected to form the OECD blacklist of countries that it would be prudent for governments and legitimate institutions to regard with at least a certain amount of caution, if not to be avoided altogether, in terms of their being uncooperative tax havens.

Other countries, those that failed to comply with two of the three guidelines, could expect to find themselves on the OECD grey list. Nauru was one of nine countries that, in April 2016, could have found itself on this list of nefariousness. Nauru? Hardly anybody even knew where Nauru was. Yet it should have come as little or no surprise that this tiny Pacific nation, flying under the international legal radar, the tropical getaway radar, the everyday trivial pursuit question radar and any other radar attuned to uncovering unknown destinations anywhere on the planet, should be involved in illicit activities on a grandiose scale. Nauru has a history of dubiety on a personal, local and national scale stretching back way into the last century.

Like many primitive nations, Nauru owes much of its social corruption to its exposure to Europeans. When the British first contacted the island in 1798, they found the natives to be friendly and easy-going. As a result, the island was referred to as 'Pleasant Island' for many decades and was used increasingly frequently as a stop-off point for fresh produce and water by European traders. Trading between the indigenous people and the passing Europeans inevitably led to the adoption of the worst of the Westerners' traits which, in turn, fuelled an internal war between the twelve local families, or clans, attributable to the uptake of alcohol and firearms as part of the general commerce with the West. Fast forward to the beginning of the twentieth century and the social corruption gives way to lessons in business and financial corruption.

Phosphate was accidentally discovered on the island (a piece of fossilised wood, used as a doorstop, turned out to be high-grade phosphate rock) in 1900 and was commercially mined and exported six years later. The phosphate was found to be of incredibly high quality and the entire island seemed to be made from it. Naturally, the British company involved spent no time in debating the merits of strip mining the accessible parts of the island once they'd secured the mining rights from Germany (Germany had 'owned' the island since 1886 under the terms of an Anglo-German agreement) and they commenced the systematic destruction of the natural habitat in search of ever-increasing profit. By 1919, a further agreement had been signed to establish the British Phosphate Commission and four years later the League of Nations decreed that Australia should act as a trustee of Nauruan welfare by restoring the land and water lost to mining on the island. New Zealand and Britain were to be co-trustees, and compensation was to be paid for all mining-related environmental damage. As a hitherto innocent society, albeit with the firearms- and booze-driven internecine war in its recent history, it's hardly surprising that the local population should pick up on the habits of a more sophisticated cohort, especially one that seemed steeped in wealth. Locals were employed by the mining consortium and would have had access to all manner of information in relation to 'maximising return on investment'.

As part of the dissolution of global empires in the mid-twentieth century, Nauru became self-governing in 1966 and by 1968 was the world's smallest republic, a remarkable achievement for a people that had twice been on the verge of extinction altogether. Two years later, in 1970, Nauru bought all the rights to the phosphate business from Australia for the sum of $AU21m – a bargain price for a commodity that was bringing in an annual revenue of between $AU100m – $AU120m at the time. Nauru was on a financial roll. Less than twenty years on and the Nauru government sued their Australian counterpart for failure to remedy the environmental damage caused by the near destruction of the island. Money was flowing in from all sides.

So, rich, self-governing and seemingly financially impregnable, Nauru had to decide what it would do with its vast wealth. A trust was established to administer amounts of money that were mind-boggling to outsiders. Per capita, Nauru was the second richest nation on earth after oil-rich Saudi Arabia. Investment was undertaken with more enthusiasm than expertise: an airline was set up, property bought and ostentatious lifestyles adopted. In Australia, Nauru bought their flagship property, Nauru House, in Melbourne; in the Philippines, they bought the Manila Pacific Star Hotel; in Guam, the Pacific Star Hotel; in the US, Pacific House in Washington, the Singer Building in Houston and Hillside Property in Oregon. To finalise all these deals, government officials undertook excessive international travel during which they flaunted their fathomless wealth.

However, the end of the primary mining on the island in the 1990s resulted in no cash flow, no reserves and no option but to succumb to asset seizure. The airline folded. Properties around the world were sold off or repossessed by lending institutions. Nauru House, the flagship of a juvenile nation playing in the toyshop of international finance, was sold to Queensland Investment Corporation in 2004. Nauru was back where it started – almost. Broke, internationally vilified, egotistically bruised, the island nevertheless held onto three significant assets: an acquired taste for wealth with accompanying arrogance, a developing understanding of large-scale corruption and secondary mining.

The first of these assets was partially assuaged in 2006 by the signing of a deal whereby Nauru received AU$40m from Australia to accommodate an influx of refugees. As a part of the deal, Australia also agreed to 'clean up the corruption' on the island. Irony notwithstanding, this looked like a good deal for Nauru, even if AU$40m is not a lot of money; further increments could surely be negotiated for future waves of refugees or even for the continued housing of the same original refugees. Meanwhile, the second asset was used effectively in a government-driven scheme to provide investor passports to foreigners who wished, for whatever reason, to have dual passport capabilities. This was a blatant passports-for-sale scheme designed to bring in more cash to the starving island. (It is noticeable that, while money never seemed to be a problem for Nauruan officials – and their families, courtesy of the trickle-down effect – ordinary and unconnected Nauruans lived in abject poverty.) Much of the scammed passport money came from two main sources: Russian-organised crime and Hong Kong drug money. These two entities also made significant investments in Nauru through bank deposits.

Secondary mining involves the mining of tailings discarded from the first round of strip mining on the island, and it continues to a dwindling extent today. It is not entirely unusual to drive the haul road and find sixty-foot-diameter craters, twenty feet deep in the actual road where, the day before, there was only road. Outsize vehicle tyres mark the deviation in the route.

For corruption to work, it was necessary for government officials (either singly or in collusion with others) to exercise a degree of control.

In January 2014, the president of Nauru, Baron Waqa sacked Peter Law and Geoffrey Eames, Nauru's sole magistrate and the chief justice respectively.

In May and June 2014, Waqa suspended five members of the opposition for criticising the Nauru government to foreign media.

In June 2015, three further opposition members were arrested and imprisoned for 'trying to destabilise' the government, again by talking to the foreign media.

Further examples of the fickle and mercenary attitudes of the Nauru government can be established by looking at its association with China and Taiwan. Both countries (China and Taiwan) seek UN support in their respective claims for dependence and independence, and they are prepared to pay for that support. Nauru plays off each against the other, depending on its needs at the time, so that Nauru will vote in favour of one or the other as it sees fit.

The following would appear to be established facts.

1980: Nauru established official relations with Taiwan.

2002: Nauru established official relations with China by offering the 'solemn recognition' of the 'One China' policy. Taiwan immediately severed all relations with Nauru and accused China of buying Nauru's allegiance for a multimillion-dollar pay-off. (Australian media investigations support this contention, pointing out that the Nauruan government was almost destitute.)

2003: Nauru closed its Beijing embassy.

2005: Nauru re-established relations with Taiwan, who became Nauru's second-biggest trading partner. In return, Nauru provided UN support in Taiwan's bid to join the UN. As a further sweetener, Taiwan provided a team of specialist doctors to work at the Republic of Nauru Hospital. China immediately severed all relations with Nauru.

2011: Wikileaks asserted that Taiwan pays a monthly stipend to certain Nauru government ministers for their continued support at the UN. It also provides a resident medical team to Nauru on a five-year renewable contract.

So this is the country with which Australia is happy to entrust the lives of some of the world's most vulnerable people, refugees. And when we say 'Australia', we mean the Australian government acting on behalf of the people. A little investigation, however, should shed doubt on whether Australia should be happy about colluding with a proven duplicitous and corrupt foreign entity: if Nauru can barely be trusted with the well-being of helpless others, how much better is Australia within the same consideration? Consider Australia's secrecy laws in relation to the whole refugee situation. These laws rightly regulate the disclosure of official information when appropriate public interest is at play: no one would reasonably argue that sensitive security files should be routinely made available to either the press or to individuals. Similarly, it would be reasonable to prevent personal information being distributed if that information could cause a security breach. However, without the visibility of certain information, it is impossible for the general public – the voters who determine who should govern – to hold the elected members to account. Consider the following extract from, *Right Now, Human Rights in Australia:*

> Secrecy laws also have implications for journalists who receive leaked material. Think, for example, of the Nauru files – a set of more than 2,000 incident reports from the Nauru detention centre exposing incidents of self-harm, sexual assaults, child abuse and violence. This reporting is crucial to informed public debate; without it, we don't know what the government is doing in our name. Any law that could criminalise the publishing of this material warrants serious concern.
>
> Currently, the Crimes Act 1914 (Cth) contains two offences that criminalise breaches of secrecy obligations; that is, they introduce criminal sanctions to obligations that Commonwealth officers already owe. Section 79 criminalises the disclosure of official secrets, and is punishable by seven years in prison. Section 70 is much broader. This section criminalises unauthorised

disclosure of any fact a Commonwealth officer has learned or any document they have obtained by virtue of their position that they are under a duty not to disclose. Breach of this provision can result in up to two years imprisonment.

This, of course, brings a number of points to the fore. Firstly, reporting on Nauru by journalists is hampered by the cost of a visa. Media visas for Nauru have been reported to cost as much as AU$15,000 each, although requests are usually refused out of hand. Obviously, the result of this is that reporting on conditions and practices on the island is virtually impossible, except when those on the ground release information at huge personal risk: two years' imprisonment is not an insignificant time, except when compared to the four and five years that the Nauru refugees spend on the island. Secondly, as Australia usually blindly follows the US, it might be worth reminding ourselves of the Supreme Court judgement in the case of the *Washington Post*'s position re Watergate: the judgement said in plain terms that 'the press is there to serve the governed, not the governors'. How can the press undertake to serve anyone if it is denied the information it requires to question the (non-security-related) actions of the government? Thirdly, a quote from Immigration Minister Peter Dutton: 'Somebody once said to me that we've got the world's biggest collection of Armani jeans and handbags up on Nauru waiting for people to collect it when they depart.'

Is that comment an unauthorised disclosure of information learned by virtue of his position that he is under a duty not to disclose because it is dysphemic? It is also, as it happens, a) absolutely incorrect and b) irrelevant: what Dutton (and others) seem to forget is that refugees are not criminals, they are not members of the Poor Clares. Refugees have precisely the same status as Dutton, though without a country to call their own, and they can wear whatever they can afford.

Information about Nauru

Information is hard to come by on Nauru. When I let colleagues and others know that I was interested in stories, rumours, case histories concerning the Nauruan environment, I was met with muted enthusiasm: everyone I spoke to thought the idea was both great and necessary, and they promised to supply me with tales of terrifying goings-on.

During my final six weeks on the island, I started pressing those who claimed to have stories to tell, but the only real help I received was from refugees. Their stories appear in the following pages under a variety of guises: How to get to Nauru, Naurumours and some of the poems. All the other information came from my own observation.

Some stories never made the cut. Towards the end of my contract, there were donation bins into which we could drop clothing or utensils or whatever to be shared out among the refugees. These bins were located in the accommodation blocks, they were locked and had large postbox-type holes cut into them for the purpose of depositing the donated items. One morning I was walking back to my room for some forgotten item and I saw two cleaners (local Nauruan employees) with their arms deep inside one of the bins, removing the donated items intended for refugees. When they saw me, they laughed and continued to steal from the bin. I could, of course, have reported this to higher management but experience told me that nothing would happen: I'd been told early on in my tenure that 'you never know who a local is related to' and that being critical of anyone could lead to your visa being cancelled. This was such a commonplace story that I decided not to include it in the body of this work. I have, however, included a story of visa cancellation, as the scale and cause of it is astounding. Yet still nothing is done at the highest levels. Variations of some of the other stories not to make the cut have been reported in the *Guardian* and elsewhere, so don't warrant repeating.

Finally, in no particular order, I thank the following people for their encouragement and/or friendship during my time on the island: Mehdi, Nasrat, Abdi, Nima, Katy, Shahin, Erica, Ibrahim, Hakima, Abas, Razieh, Baqer, Arash, David and the three expats (you know your names).

Enjoy. Think. Join the debate.

JM

...and a new road
How to get to Nauru #1

Where the wavewall rises to the sky
and scrapes the dark with a jarring thunderous threat,
the ambered moment sets in sudden, silent pause:
a moment twin-dimensioned, held within the confines of a past
inhabited by a shifting turbulence of lives
and an empty future burdened by the debt
of hope. So, the anaesthetic soundless moment roars
unheard by those whose every moment is their last.

Behind the wave, a fluid state of persecution:
the nightime raids that torture follows –
electro-probes, cigarette burns, the casual raping –
visited indiscriminate on men and women, young and old.
Relief is found only in soundproofed, screaming execution
that the blind-eyed Western world is prepared to swallow
as factional exaggeration (even though there's no escaping
the ever-growing missing lists that continually unfold).

Ahead, survival – in a world defined by mute indifference
like the invisibility of shadow under cloud.
Maybe civilisation will be reclaimed in a café coffee cup
or on a bus ride along dull and ordinary roads…

Or maybe, when the Jericho wave annihilates all chance
of wild-imagined choices, when the boat is ploughed
beneath the water, overturned and bottomed-up,
the endgame is Nauru. And all life, at last, implodes.

Coming in to Pleasant Island
How to get to Nauru #2

A cliché jewel in a vast unending sea –
      (wave-nudged reef,
            then sand-coloured beach
                  with palms and scattered beachside huts).

The plane banks right, levels, comes in straight,
lands and taxis to a halt, shuts
off its engines while wise-eyed passengers wait
to disembark, collect their bags, prepared to see…

a festrous scab on a toxic poisoned ocean;
the gnarl-black reef; up-close sand a pallid grey;
putrid palms –
      and the huts are homes.

The grounded eye is clearer than the eye in motion.
It sees the filth, the squalor and decay,
the rotting flesh that hangs off rotting bones.

A broken sonnet befitting a broken ideal which, in fact, has nothing to do with ideals, but has everything to do with a need to find justification for what is not ideal.

Nauru, First Impressions

Songs – there are none.
The singing lies
lost beneath rough tailings
when the greed has gone
from everywhere but their eyes.
So, no one sings.

And only children laugh,
through stinging days
of mindless heat
and flyblown snot.
Lives lived by half,
unknowing of the ways
that even the freshest meat
will quickly rot.

Naurumour #1

The charter flight from Brisbane to Nauru is cold. Inside the plane, the air con is turned up so high that the regular passengers – those who know – grab blankets from the overhead bins before they've even reached their seats. Anyone making the trip for the first time realises the necessity of wrapping themselves in a blanket only after there are none left, and nothing more than stoicism gets them through the flight.

Four-and-a-half hours after take-off, the plane banks above the tropical paradise of the Republic of Nauru, levels out and lands in 31-degree heat.

A number of first impressions mark these early moments on the island: the seasonless heat, constant month in, month out (although you don't realise this on your first landing); the surprising strength of the breeze that hits you at the top of the aeroplane steps like the blast from a bread oven, though yeastless and unappetising at the end of a grit-eyed flight at 13.30 on a Thursday afternoon; the waving palm fronds and other greenery that hold the promise of balmy tropical nights.

And then you're down the steps and onto the tarmac, walking to the airport building and your first taste of an exotic new place.

From the air, the compact airport building, economically planed and angled, clean lined in the tropical light, looks quasi-modern in a minimalist efficient way. But the arrivals area puts that notion to bed as soon as you enter it. There's something quite symbolic about stepping from the blindingly bright sunlight into the narrow, dark and airless corridor where you queue in twin lines before the two uniformed immigration officials waiting to sanction your entry. Immigration takes far longer either than you expect (travelling internationally has accustomed you to multi-channelled, well-staffed systems) or than is necessary (in Nauru, officialdom runs at a less than sedate pace; the result of indifference, boredom and unsmiling bureaucratic superciliousness). When your visa has been minutely scrutinised, your passport stamped, the stamp hand-notated and your passport returned, you round the corner to the baggage reclaim area – an open-ended space into which the baggage trolleys are dragged by hand and where they are manually unloaded with all bags being placed, according to size, either onto the ground or onto a long bench ready for collection. No fancy carousels here. In August 2017, a new scanning machine was installed in the baggage reclaim area and all luggage, including hand luggage, is handballed through the scanner by uninterested workers who seem unsure as to why they're performing the task.

On the other side of heavy-duty rubber doors, the arrivals hall squats in sordid squalor. A few plastic seats are bolted to the floor, a grimy café wafts deep-fried aromas of chicken and burgers into the air, a Nauru Airlines office is shut. There is nothing attractive or appealing about Nauru's airport. The floor is grubby. Grimy. Unattended except by company personnel waiting to conduct a one-on-one handover.

The FIFO workers head for the small fleet of beat-up Mercedes buses and take their seats while management pick up their car keys and find their allocated cars in the small car park. Some buses have working air con, others have open windows that don't even come close to cooling down the interior, but do allow the hot air to flow through the interior of the vehicle, so that it feels a little less hot than it actually is. On my first swing, I found myself sitting next to Len, a friendly older guy who worked in the mess.

– You'll need to buckle-up. Caught not wearing a seat belt, you get fired on the spot.

– Seriously?

– Yup.

I clicked the seat belt in place. It sprang open. I clicked it again. It sprang open.

– Just hold it across your chest. You'll be good.

Eventually, the bus pulled away, heading east into the early afternoon. We followed the road that circled the single runway and rode alongside the shore for a few minutes. The waves broke over a hidden reef about a hundred metres off the beach and the lagoon between reef and land was populated by a scattering of dolmens or coral boulders, all black. They looked like the Twelve Apostles along the Great Ocean Road, but in miniature. And in mirrored repetition: there were hundreds of them.

I turned to Len.

– Result of the mining. Pinnacles. They're all over the island.

Once away from the shoreline, we drove past occasional houses that looked semi-derelict or half-built or half-demolished. Shanty homes you might expect in the worst districts of Johannesburg or Soweto. I discovered later that these were the homes of ordinary Nauruans and each had at least one four-wheel drive and a small motorbike parked nearby. Some had several vehicle wrecks in the front yard, too, rusting and wheel-less and reflective of the buildings they guarded, as though building and vehicle shared a dignity in decay. And there were loose packs of feral dogs along the road, and on the road, and lounging in the shade off the road. Some dogs seemed to belong to the houses they wandered near to but most seemed just to inhabit the hot space they moved through, belonging to nobody and to no place. They slunk from shade to shade, unhurried, looking over their shoulders to keep an eye on the cars and buses and motorbikes sliding past them, each wearing an expression similar to that of the immigration officers at the airport: bored, slightly surly, to be given as wide a berth as possible. In reality, I came to understand, the dogs were pretty safe from traffic as there's a fifty kilometres an hour speed limit on the island and almost all drivers abide by it meticulously, the majority barely exceed forty kilometres an hour and many drive at a much lower speed. In fact, the only speeding cars I ever saw on the island were being driven by expat FIFO workers – the only people who ever seemed to be in a hurry on Nauru.

Among the houses – and often next to the houses – were what looked like abandoned forty-foot sea containers, some rusted, others apparently newer and in better condition. Many were obviously used as sheds and many more were tacked onto the main building as a kind of windowless extension to the residence. Inside the containers must have felt like the inside of an oven. Some of the containers, I noticed, were functioning as shops, with one or two, usually Chinese, men squatting outside, smoking. With no windows, the inside of the shops was too dark to make out anything in passing from the bus, even if we were travelling at low speed, so there was no way of telling at a glance what each shop sold. I guessed you'd have to wander in and look around before you'd have any real idea of the nature of the shop: grocer, hardware, dog butcher… But apart from their use as sheds, extensions and shops, the proliferation of sea containers was astounding and, the further we drove, the more astounding it became. By the time we turned off the coastal road at the Od'n hotel corner and headed inland to the centres, I estimated I'd seen at least a hundred, most empty and unused. On the internal road (the haul road, so named because it was used to haul the phosphate from the strip mines to the port) there were even more sea containers: in scrapyards, beside the road and wedged in among the trees, where it looked like they'd been for aeons so that the trees grew around them and through them and integrated them into the dendrological landscape.

And where there were no sea containers, there were abandoned motor vehicles: cars and vans and utes in various states of decay were piled up alongside the unmetalled road and beside the sparse housing in that part of the island. With a total population on Nauru in the region of ten thousand people, it looked as though each one had owned a plurality of vehicles, each of which had died and been left where it had expired, possibly as a reminder of the vast wealth enjoyed by Nauru fifty years ago. Possibly as a belligerent token of natural indolence and an uncaring attitude towards the environment.

– A few years ago, there was a plan to clear all this crap away.

Len had seen me staring at the dereliction ornamenting the side of the road and he could probably hear the internal monologue babbling in my head. Either that or every first-timer asks the question sooner or later and he just thought he'd pre-empt the asking.

— Someone with Japanese connections, apparently. The Japanese government contacted the GON — the government of Nauru — and offered to clean up all the scrap metal on the island. They were going to pay six million bucks to Nauru for the privilege and they'd send a boat over and load it up and take it back to Japan. Recycling and all that.

— Sounds like a good plan.

— It would take months but. If the GON went for it.

— Did they?

— Of course. Six million's a good amount of money to an economy going bust. And (Len's voice dropped so that no one else could hear what he said) you'd expect most of it would find its way into the pockets of a few at the top. Maybe into one pocket.

Before I'd accepted my job with the company, I'd done a bit of research into Nauru and I'd found a fair bit of corruption historically attached to the island, so I wasn't particularly surprised to hear what Len was saying. But I kind of thought that it would all be in the past or that it would exist only on a level far below that of senior governmental dealings with an international power like Japan. So, while I wasn't surprised at the action (the stealing of part or all of six million dollars), I was a little surprised at the brazenness (the involvement of a country such as Japan, which sets so much store by 'face' and integrity).

— So, how come all the containers and stuff are still here?

The way that Len was telling it sounded like this deal was recent, not ancient, history: surely the Japanese hadn't been and gone and all this debris had accumulated since then… How much time would it take to repopulate the island with so much junk? Decades, I'd have thought.

— Well, that's the point. The deal was agreed. All signed and ready to go and the boat sailed from Japan and everything. They must have done all their calculations to work out the value of the scrap. Smart people, the Japs. Anyway, it must have been well worth it for them to set it all up.

– I still don't get –

– Well, before the boat arrived and before anything could be done, the GON – or someone from the GON – told the Japs that they'd have to pay twelve million –

– But I thought you said six –

– Exactly. But someone, somewhere decided that six million wasn't enough.

– So, the Japanese said –

– Nothing. The Japs don't negotiate that kind of thing. There'd been a deal and now the deal had been broken. Without another word, the ship turned around and sailed back to Japan.

– So Nauru, or someone in the Nauru government, not only didn't get their greedy twelve mill, they lost the original six?

The bus was turning into the gate at Regional Processing Centre One (RPC1) where security guards came on board to check ID passes, so Len said nothing more. He just smiled at me and he smiled at the guard and he sat back against his seat as the bus entered the centre that would be home for us and everyone else on the buses for the next three weeks. It looked like the camps depicted on TV and it looked like a cross between a prison compound and a construction depot because of the heavy vehicles parked inside the fence near the gate.

The place seemed to be deserted apart from two incongruous roosters strutting across the hard stone ground a few metres in front of the bus. Slowly, we disembarked, climbed down into the roosters' domain, collected out bags and headed towards one of the buildings for a fly-in briefing.

As we walked through the sweltering heat, Len turned to me and smiled.

– Greed and stupidity, he said. You'll see plenty of that.

Locals

Beachside birthed beneath fringed
infertile palms, the children reap
the island's mineral wealth, tinged
with Midas lifestyles, they think it's theirs to keep.

Let the wet season wash away the wishes
of the hopeful, let it sweep
their summer dreams far out to where the fishes
wait in shadowed depths beyond the reef.
Let the blazing months sear away the visions
of false futures, let them peel
away the onion skins of options, of decisions
wrapped in innocence. There's a real
world waiting in front of every ageing face:
a half per cent of one per cent will ever leave this place

Another broken sonnet to reflect the broken notion of Nauru's identity. In the 1970s, Nauru was the second richest country on earth, after oil-rich Saudi Arabia, by virtue of its natural deposits of high-grade phosphate. Today (in 2018) the locals retain the arrogance of unearned wealth and, despite the rampant and blatant poverty that blankets almost all the island, they continue to live in denial: they are on the cusp of starvation and their only hope lies in the Australian government's ongoing payment for the country to house refugees. The Nauruans need to know that their time is limited unless they change their attitude. To do that, they would need to change their culture. It's not going to happen.

Nauru Refugee Blues #1

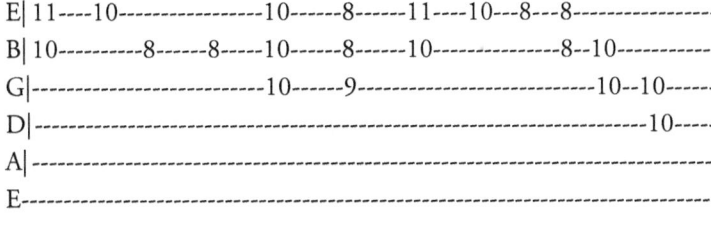

I woke up this morning, dust all around my bed.
Said, I woke up this morning, I found dust all around my bed.
If I don't leave here soon, gonna wake up someday dead.

My baby, he didn't make it, went down in the cold, grey sea.
Said my baby he didn't make it, he gone down in the cold, cold sea.
When I leave this lonesome prison, he'll be waiting there for me.

We're running and a-crying, the police is chasing fast.
Yeah, we was running, we was crying. The police was chasing fast.
If they'd done catched us, baby, I believe we breathe our last.

We gone out on the ocean, a hundred riding high.
I said we went out on the ocean, a hundred riding high.
If we could reach Australia, no one have to die.

The engine it ain't working, hard waves bearing down.
I said the engine it ain't working and the hard waves coming down.
Took my baby to the water – I believe I watched him drown.

They brung us to this island, there's fever makes you ill.
Yeah, they put us on an island where fever'll make you ill.
If the dengue doesn't get you the phosphate surely will.

Got a Nauru visa, what I got to lose?
I said I got a twenty-year Nauru visa, there's nothing left to lose.
We're living in a hellhole with the Nauru refugee blues.
I said I'm dying in this hellhole, got the Nauru refugee blues.

Horse trading with the US

They've all gone now.
To Shitsville Mississippi
and Nowhere Arkansas
and Deadend South Dakota.
All? Stand them in a row:
twenty-nine – a pathetic quota
taken from a thousand-plus waiting for
a visa to some false ideal – a happy
vision of a movie life.

Imaginations, let loose on Hollywood
dreams, dream toothpaste smiles,
Miami suits and east-coast class.
But while the dreams are rife
with cushion-seated, movie-pass
enactments, monochrome reality denies
anything even remotely as good.

An uncaring, bare-board room.
A one-horse, dust-bowl desert town.
Food tokens (with cat's-cradle strings attached).
Limits on where to go and what to do.

But at least it's not a hovel in Khartoum
With mortar shells and misery pressing down.
Maybe refugees and their new lives are ill-matched
But, *inshallah*! It's not the nightmare of Nauru.

inshallah: an expression of Arabic Islamic origin that translates as 'God willing'

In the Heart of Darkness

Woken by the roar of nightrain
on the roof, a fifteen-minute
deluge of relief augmenting
outside the indoor air con
before the morning heat again.
But for now, a cool room, and in it
barely broken sleep before everything
quietens quickly towards dawn.

In the camps, the storm sends rats
into the tents where crowded people sleep;
rats that search out meagre food…that
hole dropped clothes or final shoes; cheap
but rare possessions in a place
where rats and lesser people share a space.

Expats live in purpose-built, breeze-block and brick accommodation: showers, en suite bathrooms, a fridge in every room. Asylum seekers and refugees who live in the processing centres (RPC2 and RPC3), live in tents that house up to forty single men in each. No air conditioning, no fridge, no fans. When the tropical storms hit, they bring welcome relief from the unbearable heat, but they also bring the rats that seek shelter from the sudden violent weather. Usually, the storms last fifteen to twenty minutes (although they are often repeated several times during a single night) but fifteen to twenty minutes is easily long enough for rats to invade.

Naurumour #2

— Before we get into the agenda, I just want to clarify what you might've heard on the grapevine. Off the record.

The weekly meeting in the conference room was about to start: the six-strong management team, two women, four men, shuffled notebooks and coffee cups down both sides of the table while the departmental manager rested his forearms on the table, twined his hands together as though about to pray, and smiled his split melon smile at no one in particular. To his left, Saed stared at his laptop screen ready to take the minutes in his slightly-better-than-pidgin English that occasionally resulted in humorous or ambiguous statements. It didn't matter: nobody ever really read the minutes – they were for the record only, to satisfy Australian Border Force (ABF) requirements.

The room itself was functional: long enough to accommodate the series of tables jigsawed together to form a continuous board for twenty people, nine or ten along each side, a projector fixed to the ceiling over the centre of the table, its cables loosely taped into a knot of contained confusion directly below, a roll-down screen attached to the wall at the far end of the room. Chairs flanked the table and spare chairs were pushed against the walls. The air con scythed cold air through the assembled bodies with a vicious force that rapidly cooled the coffee in the cups.

— So, off the record.

Saed sat back, folded his arms and continued to stare at the laptop screen. He'd been at the morning briefing meetings and he'd heard the rumours before. Elsewhere, the chat and banter slowed to a stop until everyone had turned towards the head of the table.

— You've probably heard that Wilson sent two people home yesterday.

Brief nods and pens tapped on notebooks and an air of anticipation. Everyone had heard what had happened as soon as it had happened and the talk for the next hour or two had been of nothing else. There were few details available at the time, though, and all anyone knew for sure was that two security guards had been shipped out for visa irregularities. Additional information would be welcome.

*

There are two levels of security on the island: Wilson Security ran the top tier – the actual security – while a local firm, as decreed by the GON, worked under Wilson guidance, but not under their control. The local guys ran the sign-in books at the processing centre gates and acted as a presence outside the activity tents. Whenever there was an incident in one of the tents, they did nothing. The arrangement with the locals had been put in place by the GON almost certainly as a means of providing sinecure employment for islanders, employment paid for by Australian taxpayers. As far as reputations went, Wilson Security was respected by almost everyone (only one guard was loathed by some refugees for historical instances of bullying, lack of compassion, brutality) while the locals were despised by almost everyone, being seen as lazy, untrustworthy and thieving.

*

– Well, what happened was, the head of Wilson got a call from someone in the GON to say that a local was coming back to the island and he would be working for Wilson –

– Coming back from where?

– Not sure. Just 'coming back'. Anyway, Wilson said, 'Okay, send us his details so we can do the usual background checks and so on.' The details arrived pretty quick and the head of Wilson phoned the GON within the hour.

He paused to sip at his cooling coffee and the rest of the room followed suit as if they'd been waiting for his signal before they drank.

– So he called them back and said words to the effect that 'Your boy is not going to work for us. Not today, not tomorrow. Not ever.' We don't know what was in the information they'd been given, but it must have been pretty bad –

– Maybe he'd been inside, onshore.

– That was what was suspected but we don't know. Anyway, two hours later, Wilson gets a call, again from the GON, to say that they – the GON – had recently conducted random immigration checks and they'd found that two Wilson guards had visa irregularities and would have to leave the island immediately.

Fake indignation rattled around the room. Fake, because this was not something out of the blue, not something they'd known nothing about; fake, because it was salacious rumour based on corrupt governmental attitudes that hadn't come as a surprise; fake, because it was a good story that would stand many a retelling.

The manager let the rumbling die down.

– The GON also found irregularities in the visa of one of our chefs. So, he's gone.

– What? What's the point of that? I mean, I get the payback with Wilson, but –

– We employ Wilson Security, they're contracted to us, so we also have to bear the brunt. Feel the pain. So we can bring pressure to bear.

– And will we?

– No. Wilson doesn't care. They'll just redeploy their guys to Manus or to wherever.

– And the chef?

– He'll be okay

– Hey, maybe the food'll improve.

*

The following week, further 'random immigration checks' apparently uncovered two more Wilson Security personnel with visa irregularities.

They were deported from Nauru on the first available flight, which happened to be the next day. No one else from any other company was found to have the same problem. Wilson Security accepted the situation and continued to refuse to succumb to GON pressure to employ their unemployable nominee.

Soon thereafter, three members of the Wilson Security contingent were allegedly found to have similar problems with their visas, visas issued by the GON in the first place, and, because there was no flight off the island for four days, the Wilson staff members were imprisoned in the island's high-security jail until departure time. Wilson Security responded by informing the GON that, while it was within the rights of the GON to exercise this level of punitive behaviour under the guise of tightened immigration control, any further such action would trigger the agreement that the GON would be responsible for replacing the deported individuals. And not from their own cache of dubious characters, either.

No further deportations occurred because of visa problems and Wilson Security still maintained its control over who it employed. If you stand up to a bully, he'll usually back down.

Any Hamid or Muhammed or

He scuffs a path through another day of dust,
the burden of his thinking held hard on calloused feet.

Fifteen friendless years of age with just
himself, his fenced-in thoughts, a rage of heat
and little else to speed his progress through
the world. Ten thousand miles and then…
the dream of a Netflix life…? Somewhere new…?
or a Nauru visa for twenty years, when
he'll be thirty-five and old, having lost
his boyhood before his empty adult years
spread his stone-dry living across
a nihilistic future that screams isolation in his ears.

But his best years aren't behind him, they're still ahead:
the uncountable eternity of being finally dead.

Recreation

The Greenlight kava bar where a dirty
dish of dirty dreams costs no more than
a moment's work for us, a half day
labour for the local men.

(A scant-tooth dribbler wears a shirt he
smears filthy fingers of both hands on.
He grins a wet-slack lip, the play
of bulbous features broken.)

No pleasure. No words. Just a gradual
numbing of the lips. Then the tongue and
then the throat. Until the dreams

are gone and only some residual
earthen gravetaste is left behind.
The night is done, it seems.

Asylum seekers on Nauru

I

No one is writing their history.
No one is listening to their heartbeat.
No one is trying to unravel the mystery
of their pain, their fear, or their defeat.

No one calls them by their name.
No one talks to their inner thoughts.
No one is asking why they came
through boiling waters in death boats.

No one gives them more than food.
No one reaches into their lonely hell.
No one is assessing their change in mood
from human, or less than human, to an empty shell.

I am me! I will be you!
I am god and I am breath.
I'm not a number, not someone who
walks complicit on the road to death.
I will be me and not a shadow who
walks complicity on the road to death.

II

Cuff their wrists with rusted velour
and stop their mouths with cadmium lace:
the procession in the clouded mirror
will pass beyond each haggard face.

Bind their eyes with barbed-wire ribbon
and ring their necks in satin rope:
once relinquished, forever given –
vale freedom, vale hope.

March 2018: recent reports have highlighted the mental health problems encountered by asylum seekers on Nauru. Doctors who have worked on the island contradict claims by the Australian government that the available care is adequate and sufficient: Plainly, it is not. There are no psychologists qualified in the treatment of mental trauma to attend to cases such as the recent instance in which a twelve-year-old girl, threatening extreme self-harm, was deemed to be under adequate supervision from 'several healthcare options'. Asylum seekers are among the most vulnerable people on the planet: Australia is failing those on Nauru. They deserve better.

It didn't happen that way

Overnight, the rain came in.
At first, death quiet
and unnoticed
like the onset of old age
or the emergence of the grave itself
morphing from the mist.
But then, the onrush of invading
noise, a loudness so high it
obliterated all resist-
ence in its aural damage,
as it smashed traditional expectations
(the sudden blue sky at
a washed-clean, five a.m. dawn,
thirty-one degrees,
an onshore breeze…)

It didn't happen that way.

The rags of dawn lay dirtgrey, soiled and dank.
The still air clouded, poisonous and rank.
Downpours unpoured down hung in torrentous pause
as the softdawn ocean breath stroked whisper-distant shores.
Filthpools patched the broken road.
A simmering dengue haze
swarmed biblically then rose and flowed
towards the camps, towards the present future with all its
accumulating days.

Ceci, ce n'est pas une vie.
It's not, at least, such as we
might know it, with its easy
fluctuations to minimal degree.
This is life suspended
to which no expectations are appended
and wakeful dreams are nightmares
inescapable. And no one cares.

How we perceive a tropical island is not necessarily how a tropical island is. We expect the sudden night-time storms to herald in 'another fabulous day in paradise' but sometimes, the 'fabulous' is a veneer that hides a hazardous reality. The smiling faces on the travel agent's posters rarely portray the entirely real. On a good day, Nauru is a third world country with third world amenities and third world levels of sickness. For under-nourished, vulnerable people, health can be a precarious state. And the asylum seekers and refugees on Nauru live in a precarious state of health.

The room

Fresh from their three-week respite, the case workers approach the settlement. The moonscape excavations, metres from the scant shanties, gape like cavities in the rotten teeth of the terrain and the houses themselves look like the next teeth to succumb to the rotting. The case workers park the four-wheel drive beside the unused community noticeboard and walk the ten paces to the house through stinking heat. They knock on the flaking paint of the front door and wait. No one comes in answer to their knocking and they try again. Again, no one comes. They push gently at the door and it swings open onto the darkness inside and they enter the unwelcoming space with the confidence of having been here many times before and they head directly for the bedroom where the know they'll find…

The room smells of dust. Years of decay – deliberate and denigrating years of denial and uninterest – have laid a fetid grey-brown patina over the air so that the very breathing of it seems solid with its clogging. Newer scents fight for recognition: stale breath, sweat, the sweet yet sour flavour of soiled garments. But they fight mostly in vain. The stink of half a decade holds at bay these *nouveaux saveurs* in much the same way as the darkened walls stave off the light that tries to find a way into the room through the grimed and gritted window. The faded curtain – half closed, unthreaded, the colour of dust and as insubstantial – gravels the sun's efforts and shields the light inside as a uniform dinge. At night, the sodium security light – when it works – equally fails to penetrate into the interior of the dim cell.

In the far corner of the room, a filthy mattress lies on the filthy floor. Occasional movement on this rudimentary bed sends small belches of unimaginable stench into the air immediately above it, though the foul cloud lasts no more than a few seconds before it dissipates, absorbed into the general aromatic soup of the room.

A figure is half-lying on the mattress, propped against the wall, huddled beneath a heap of rags which once had been a sheet, a dress, a headscarf – but which are all now unrecognisable. Eyes, dull dark discs in phlegmy whites, are open but stare at nothing, or nothing that can be seen in the room. Staring perhaps into the memories of hope lost among the debris of the past. Or into the time before the past ever was.

The figure is female. A woman – though her gender seems of no consequence either to herself or to her surroundings – and whatever it is she sees, present in the room or otherwise, her expression betrays no emotion at the sight: she is evidently uninterested in, or else insensitive to, the implications of what is before her eyes.

Her stillness is the statuary stillness of the inanimate, an immobility heavy with the redolence of aeons even though she is no more than thirty years old, maybe less. Her head, tilted slightly towards the wall, rests half against her shoulder. Her features are hard-edged beneath taut skin, skin the colour of faded blue gum, long fossilised then longer bleached until what is left holds the sick hue of rot deep within. It is the skin of the outdoors-woman made captive in light-starved subterranean holes. Where the skin is pulled tight across cheek or chin it is almost translucent, contrasting sharply with the blue-black of her cracked lips and the blue-black miasm of her hair.

*

If the case workers stand back for a moment, if they take in the room in total, they might wonder how – and why – this woman came to be here, for there is no evidence of a life beyond the mattress; no discarded clothing, no shoes, no personal effects. And no furniture that might be hiding such things. Even taking into account the woman, the mattress, somehow the room remains essentially empty. There's a basic quality, a required nuance of something vital that is missing from the scene. The room is abandoned of all…decency. Or civilisation, anyway. This absent element allows the case workers to understand that, however she arrived in the room, it is not the way she will leave it. If she will ever leave at all. They understand perfectly well, as they know how and why the woman came here in a practical sense, although the how and why in a moral sense eludes them completely.

*

Movement on the mattress. Soft discharges of noxious vapour pouffe soundlessly upwards as the woman shifts her arm a little, trying for a more comfortable position than the one she has been in for…well, for a long time. As she moves in languid discare, she dislodges a shred of covering – a rag, a remnant – and exposes a breast, limp and empty…a crumpled sack, useless and all but forgotten in its undesirableness, the dust-black currant nipple shrivelled into the pap. The woman fails to notice her nakedness or, more likely, is uncaring of it. Her rheumy eyes continue to fix on the midpoint between squalor and eternity as she places her arm at her side curling her fingers against an emaciated hip.

And then she is still again.

Neither she nor anything else makes a sound in the room but the silence is far from easy. It is the silence of imminence, portentous, filled with dread unnamed, dread inescapable. The woman's breathing is too shallow either to be heard or to be seen in a rising and falling of the rags she lies half beneath. Had it not been for the moving of her arm, the memory of which has so quickly become unreliable…maybe an illusion…it might have been thought that… That what? That she is dead? There's something callous in the thought but something equally callous in the fact that she remains alive…

A sigh. Is it really a sigh…? Could it have been… It is a sigh. The woman moves again (once more exploding soft exudations of rancid putrescence into the air), looks down…towards the wall at her side. Her expression unchanged, her eyes remain dull. She is looking at her child, naked and unmoving beside her, its eyes as flat and dark as the eyes of its mother, its mouth open. But just a little.

*

Almost frantically, the case workers search the room again for… For anything…to connect… There's a child…child?…

…Nothing…

*

Only the olfactory offence gives any indication that an infant inhabits – or has inhabited – the room. The provenance of one of the multitude of fetid layers is instantly recognisable once the possibility is made clear; the stink of ageing excrement and urine-soaked material, a baby stink as identifiable as fingerprints, malodorous and choking.

*

Are the case workers still wondering? Or are they numbed by the scene to such an extent that they no longer regard wonder as an option? Have they grown insensitive to a degradation hitherto beyond their contemplation? Or are they still capable of being shocked, still able to ask why, albeit with inarticulate 'what abouts?' and 'how cans?'

*

The woman on the mattress, that cesspit of a mattress, septic resting place of odium, appears not to ask 'why?' or 'what about?' or 'how can?'. She appears to ask nothing, merely to accept. And in that acceptance, occasionally to look down.

The infant, soiled and reeking, asks nothing in its innocence. It lies next to its mother, neither complaining nor accepting nor aware that it has anything to complain about or to accept. It lies with open eyes and open mouth and unmoving limbs and it would be only a waste of time and speculation in trying to guess its age, the whereabouts of its father, its sex. It is no more than an infant beside its mother on a decomposing mattress in an unspeakable room.

The woman – the mother – moves again, looks down again as

though she has sensed something happening beside her. Yet her expression remains as it has always, her arm remains against her hip, her eyes retain their rheumy uninterest. Nevertheless, she looks down at her offspring, quietly witnessing nothing. Or has something changed? Has some subtle disturbance occurred within the smeared fragments of cloth heaped around the baby?

She watches almost lazily, unconcerned, without so much as a question forming in her mind. If there is a change of some sort, and if she has noticed it, she shows no sign. The child has not moved and does not move.

But something moves.

The woman – her instinct – was right… She sensed…maybe a prelude to movement…maybe a…but…

From between the child's lips a slow flicker of dark thread. Further. Longer thread vibrating.

The woman – the mother – watches impassively as the cockroach scuttles out of the infant's mouth…scuttles out…in…out again, over its chin…neck…shoulder. Gone. The woman watches the insect leave the body of her dead child and she moves her arm to a position a little more comfortable than it had been against her hip.

A senseless place to be

You can hear the quiet crying in the night,
the whispered lethe lullabies that fail
to send her simple dreams to sleep.
You can see the butter moon squat fat upon the water,
its silent laughter shaking the surface
of the sea to shore.
You can feel the turning of the earth in tight
and tighter circles, spinning on the nail
of angels, to which they cling and weep.
You can taste where drying ashes fought a
sad annihilating race
against the conflagration at her core.

But can you smell the mounting fear in her heart?
Can you smell displacement's stench that forces her apart?
Can you smell them coming closer now? It's about to start…

Wild dogs on Nauru

In the niggard shade beneath diseased trees
surly dogs lie. Expressions – part contempt,
part belligerence, but wholly mean – emanate
from rheumy eyes. Several, whelped
with empty paps where
only fleas now feed, slump heat-exhausted with dreams undreamt
in snarling vigilance against sleep's mate –
a circling death in alpha shape or else ill-health

from lack of food, tainted water or young old age.
All feral; spiv-eyed in backward glances as, moving round
the island in loose nomadic packs, they rummage
for an easy feed amongst the crap that everywhere can be found
tossed along the roadside. Chicken bones, fish heads, rice.
They steal, from children's hungry fingers, naked bread
and eat the vomit of other dogs (so eat the fish heads twice)
and on and on until, one by one, each dog lies dead.

By then, they've bred some more. Their cycle spins
while, inside dark houses, locals eat their chicken, rice and fish.
They have their kids and lie around beneath slow-churning
fans and die before their time; diabetic, coronaried, obese.
As each life prematurely ends, an innocent life begins.
And so it goes, with increased expectancy as ethereal as a wish
in a place unused to habit's change, where learning
rarely happens and the breeding of the dogs will never cease.

The story goes that a veterinary group, styled along the lines of *Medecins sans Frontières*, offered to come to Nauru. Their mission was to sterilise those dogs on the island whose owners wanted them to be sterilised, and to euthanise the packs of wild dogs that roam the country. Wild dogs have attacked and killed a number of people over the years (notably someone in a wheelchair and a young toddler, both within the past two years) and, despite being largely lethargic, are occasionally aggressive. The Nauruan

How to get to Nauru #3

Let's call him Malik. Malik is an eighteen-year-old Afghan boy living with his parents in Tehran, the Iranian capital. He was born in Tehran and he's lived nowhere else during his eighteen years. His father is a businessman, although what type of business is unknown, even to Malik.

There are frequent purges in Tehran: political purges, religious purges, indiscriminate purges. The police sweep an area or a neighbourhood to round up the latest undesirables, many of whom are jailed, many of whom disappear. This happens frequently enough for it to have become woven into the fabric of everyday life in Tehran and early warning systems operate by word of mouth to alert vulnerable groups whenever trouble is about to visit. Sometimes, the early warning system fails.

Malik was nearing the end of his schooldays, having completed twelve years study, and he held vague ideas of continuing his education to tertiary level. He was good with technology and he was good at maths: maybe he'd become an engineer.

---

government were interested in the proposal and allegedly asked how much the government would be paid for allowing this procedure to take place. The animal welfare group explained that there was a cost in undertaking this task, but that the cost would be borne by the welfare group. But the Nauruan government wanted to know, what's in it for us? The welfare group explained that Nauru would be free of feral dogs, the breeding of domestic dogs would be, to an extent, controlled through a sterilisation programme, and the Nauruan citizenry would be safer. But how much will you pay us, the GON asked? When it was finally established that no money would change hands – in any direction – the GON refused to sanction the deal. Dogs continue to roam the roadsides unchecked except by occasional wayward motorists, although there have been short periods when the GON has sanctioned 'dollar-a-dog' type culling programmes which result in a few dogs (feral and domestic) being slaughtered for the bounty.

Each morning, Malik would walk to school, study as hard as any other boy of his age, and walk home to his family at the end of the day. Until the day that the authorities decided to crack down on 'illegal residents' in the city, starting with the schools. Because Malik was Afghani, even though he'd been born in Tehran, he had no documentation, no rights and no official status, so, when the militia entered the school (with no early warning system alert), he knew he'd be one of those singled out for attention. What he didn't expect was what actually happened. As Malik left school, his ID was checked and, as expected, found to be inadequate. He was beaten up on the spot, thrown onto a bus and taken down town to be held in detention. No explanation, other than his being an illegal resident, was offered for his treatment, nor was any offered to any of the other detainees in the centre. Nor was there any indication of how long he would be held. There was a great number of people being held in the cells but it was impossible to know how many had been there for days or weeks and how many had just arrived: people tended not to talk much because it was known that informers were often insinuated into the mass of 'criminals' in order for the authorities to gain information they could use against other criminals, dissenters or undesirables.

We in the West read about this type of action happening in the Middle East or in Afghanistan, or Pakistan, or Somalia or elsewhere, and we deplore it. But we deplore it from a distance, a distance not only of miles, but an even greater distance of culture: we're cocooned in a comfort bubble of relative freedom protected from state interference at this level so that our response to it when we do hear about it or read about it, is purely on an intellectual basis. *In theory*, this sort of thing shouldn't be allowed to happen; *in theory*, the actions of a police state are to be roundly condemned; *in theory*, we are disgusted. Malik and his comrades didn't live in theory, they lived in the reality of it. (There are also, of course, those in the West who believe that governments wouldn't act in such a manner if it weren't necessary, that there's no smoke without fire, so the detainees must have done something…

There are also those in the West who simply turn a blind eye: it's nothing to do with me.)

The reality was that a young boy – one of many, and by no means the youngest of the group – had been separated from his family for no legitimate reason other than that of not being allowed to carry legitimate ID because of his ethnicity. Imagine this, the first step in the onset of terror.

Fortunately, Malik, like most of his generation around the world, had learned to be resourceful enough to be able to locate an illegal mobile phone among the prisoners and he persuaded the owner to let him use it to contact his parents. (When he tells the story, Malik becomes emotional whenever his parents have to be involved: his continuing love for them makes the story all the more poignant.) His father somehow managed to persuade the authorities to release his son but the release was contingent on Malik being deported to Afghanistan, his country of origin (even though he'd never lived there, never been there, and had no familiarity with either the language or the culture). Still, anywhere, even Afghanistan, surely, had to be better than detention in Tehran with all the uncertainty that that entailed.

Once he'd arrived in Afghanistan, but unsure as to exactly where in the unfamiliar country he was, Malik felt even more isolated and lost. His inability to speak the local language meant that he could barely communicate with those around him and his ignorance of everyday cultural behaviour made him stand out as an alien, a pariah of sorts who it was best to avoid. Fortunately, Malik met a stranger who spoke his language and the stranger, Abbas, agreed to help him.

Abbas took Malik to Kabul where, because it was the country's capital city, it should have possibly afforded more opportunities. But opportunities for what? Malik had no papers, still spoke no Afghani language, still felt isolated. On top of which, when he phoned home to tell his parents he was in Kabul, he discovered that his mother was sick. The sickness, caused almost certainly by the deportation of her son, was serious enough for Malik to try to get a visa that would allow him to travel back to Tehran on compassionate grounds. However, to get a visa he needed other documents… These were the documents, the lack of which had brought him into this situation, in the first place. He decided to travel illegally to Iran.

Malik moved around the city listening to people in the street, in cafés, on buses. He asked questions wherever he could and took the rebuffs with politeness and courtesy.

Eventually, he met Akbar, a taciturn man who turned out to have connections to a group of people smugglers outside the city. Akbar agreed to help and he told Malik to meet him on the outskirts of the city later that night.

The following days are a blur of confusion, sleep deprivation, disorientation and fatigue for Malik. He arrived at the agreed rendezvous and found to his surprise that Akbar was already there, waiting for him with only a backpack. Malik also carried a backpack containing spare clothes, personal items, nothing of value. With barely a word, Akbar set off away from the city of Kabul on foot with Malik following. They skirted the city's outer suburbs and, as darkness solidified around them, they walked through mountains for the entire night, moving further away from habitation and into hard desolation. Nor did the hard desolation diminish once they came out of the mountains: they were met by a group of people smugglers, as Akbar had promised, and Malik climbed into a truck, where he slept fitfully among others in the same plight. They drove for days through the desert with little water and no food until they arrived in Tehran under cover of dark. During this journey, Malik maintained as much of a silence as he could, not wanting to surrender any information or personal details that could be used against him but, at the same time, vaguely answering questions so as to appear friendly.

Back 'home', he saw his mother, who began to recover as soon as her son arrived, and he discussed his future with his family. His father knew that Malik had to leave: if he stayed in Tehran, he would be arrested again and, this time, there would be no bargaining for his release as he would effectively be a fugitive. But if he returned to Afghanistan, he would surely stand out as an outsider: the Taliban would certainly kill him because of his race, religion and education. His father had always previously resisted helping in his son's escape (except when he'd been detained in jail) because of the danger if they were caught, and because of Malik's youth: he was deemed too young to take such extreme chances away from the family home. But now his father saw how Malik was suffering, how the stay in Kabul had affected him, and how staying in Tehran was no longer possible. It was decided that Malik would travel to safety: he would go to Australia.

Malik's father knew someone in the city who could forge a passport good enough to pass through most checkpoints and he paid the requisite amount to have one made for his son. When the passport arrived, Malik's father arranged and paid for his son to fly to Kuala Lumpur in Malaysia.

The passport proved equal to Malaysian immigration and Malik arrived in KL without incident. Following instructions, he was met by a contact who drove him for three hours by car to an unknown harbour away from the city, after he'd spent twenty-four hours locked in a 'safe house' not far from the airport. The 'safe house' had held a number of people – 'more than twelve' – who were in a similar situation to Malik and when he and some of the others arrived at the harbour, they were joined by another group to total seventeen 'illegals' who were crammed aboard a speedboat that would take them to Indonesia. The trip took four-and-a-half hours across mostly calm waters at night.

Once on Indonesian soil, the following schedule occurred:

* The seventeen occupants of the speedboat were locked in a house for forty-eight hours with no food or water, no power – so no fan or other method of cooling down. The heat was unbearable and the mosquitoes more so.

* They were transferred to Jakarta, firstly by bus, despite having been told (and presumably having paid for) a transfer by plane. The bus trip took fifty-four hours. They were given no water, but, as there was no bathroom on the bus, and as the bus didn't stop at all, the lack of water possibly circumvented other problems.

* Before they reached Jakarta, they were transferred to a van, which took them to a house a further three hours away. In the house, they were given a little food and had access to a primitive shower.

* Under cover of darkness, they were driven by car for four hours to a port where they boarded a ship that would finally deliver them to Jakarta.

Since arriving in Indonesia, Malik had spent a hundred and nine hours – or a little over four-and-a-half days – locked up without adequate food, water or sanitation, surrounded by strangers – and smugglers who had little investment in the welfare of their charges. In addition to this time, the migrants now spent seventeen days locked up in yet another substandard Jakarta house, while they waited for a boat to Australia.

It didn't happen.

The boat, when it arrived, took them to an island off the coast of Indonesia. Malik believes it was the 'last island in Indonesia, the closest to Christmas Island' but he can't find it on a map. (It seems likely that the island was Pulau Padar, an island between Rinca and Komodo Islands.) He knows only that he, along with the others, was on the new island for one day, without any food or water whatsoever. They were told not to talk to anyone but they were allowed some movement outside the house – until they saw both crocodiles and Komodo dragons nearby. Everyone stayed put.

Finally, the following afternoon, another boat arrived to take them to their final Indonesian destination: they were about to sail to Australia, freedom and safety. A sense of relief overlaid the fatigue and anxiety everyone experienced, and they boarded the new boat in better spirits than they'd been in for a very long time. The boat was twenty-five metres long, was covered against the elements and had a crew of five. During the time they'd been shunted around Indonesia, the migrant numbers had grown to a hundred and eleven, and all of them now crammed into the small vessel.

By now, Malik was ill. He had contracted a sickness that caused vomiting and fever, and he'd been given some unknown medication that simply knocked him out when he boarded the craft. Fortunately, by the second day at sea, he was conscious and feeling well enough to be aware of his surroundings: his surroundings being an open sea in rough conditions, a crowded boat with little or no safety equipment, and more than a hundred desperate people, many of whom were as sick as he was. But Malik was fortunate because, as the boat began to take on water, he could at least help in the bailing out. His efforts contributed to the boat staying afloat, if only temporarily. At five a.m. the next day, the boat sank completely. His fortunes were about to change drastically.

Malik had never learned to swim.

As the boat disappeared beneath the waves, the migrants understandably panicked. Anything that could, or might, float was grabbed at, fought for, protected. Malik managed to grab onto an inner tube and, with it, he kept his head above water for seven hours. During these seven hours, he watched as a twenty-three-year-old friend had a heart attack in the water and drowned, he watched a three-year-old drown alongside his sister and both parents: Malik watched five people die in front of his eyes and he could do absolutely nothing about it.

The Australian navy picked up the survivors at the end of the seven hours in the turbulent water and landed them on Christmas Island.

Unsurprisingly, Malik had nightmares every night for more than six months. He was treated by psychologists but 'they did nothing'. He was given medication but he refused to take it for fear of becoming addicted. At eighteen years of age, Malik had to tough it out as he'd had to do so many times in his relatively short life. The eleven months he spent on Christmas Island belong to the only period in his life he won't talk about; the details of how he lived, where he lived, remain shrouded in a silence that speaks as loudly as any words might.

One day, he was among a group of nineteen migrants who were told that they were being transferred to Nauru and that they'd be processed on Nauru before being moved on to a third-party country, but that that third-party country would not be Australia. The rest of the migrants from his boat were to be transferred directly to Australia. No reasons for the split were given. Not that it mattered: Malik had been told he would be processed and he would be relocated to a safe residence. After nearly a year on Christmas Island, he was about to resume a version of life that almost amounted to 'normal' in a country where he'd be able to take up a road to a future. He was relieved, if not happy.

His future? He has been on Nauru for four years.

After an induction in RPC1, he was housed in RPC2, a camp for single men who shared accommodation in canvas tents of forty people. Malik is an incredibly polite man who refuses to become involved in action, direct or otherwise, because his father instilled in him a belief that violence, either in action or thought, is bad and can lead to no good end. He is articulate and reasonable. And it was with this mindset that he approached Australian immigration officials for information about his situation. He was told that, potentially, he would have to stay on Nauru for five years, as decreed by Scott Morrison, the then Minister for Immigration and Border Protection. The following year, Morrison had been replaced by Peter Dutton, who denied the five-year detention, declaring that Malik and those like him would stay on Nauru for ten years.

There have been some improvements during Malik's time on the island, but they are minimal. When he first moved into his shared tent in RPC2, there were no fans to either cool the temperature (even at night, the temperature never really drops below twenty-six degrees) or dispel the fetid odours of forty people being crammed into a tight space. Nor were there any personal phones (there are now – in fact, just about everyone has a mobile; but these are now refugees, people with exactly the same status as Peter Dutton, just without a country to call home). Back in 2013, the migrants had to seek permission to call home and then they had to queue for up to seven hours under the direct sun to access one of the few public phones. They were allowed ten minutes for the call, once a week. They also had to queue for up to four hours, again in the direct sun, for food that was initially okay, but which deteriorated daily. (The food in 2017 was generally more adequate, although access to fresh fruit and salads in the camps was extremely limited, while the food in RPC1, where the expats ate, was plentiful.) Malik could shower daily – but for no more than two minutes – but he had no access to washing machines to clean his clothes. All personal belongings had to be carried all day as the local security guards would quite openly steal from the tents. That is, the Nauruans, who had access to earning money and to goods and services, would openly thieve from refugees who effectively had nothing.

Nowadays? Malik is disappointed with everything, although he generally keeps his feelings to himself (as his father counselled), showing no negative emotion.

He distrusts the US deal because he has seen almost no movement in acceding to it by either party, the US or Australia. He also strongly distrusts Trump's America because he feels there's a lack of respect for refugees. All of which is moot, though: Malik is one of the few refugees who hasn't even had a US interview yet, so he's not even on the radar if the deal is put into practice. Not that this unduly disturbs him, as he doesn't really want to go to the States.*

Malik works for the expat company running the logistics on the island. A willing and flexible worker with a gentle sense of humour and a deep-rooted sense of honour.

---

* Recently, Malik has been interviewed several times by the US teams charged with vetting refugees and he is in line for consideration for a move to the States. His closest friend on Nauru left in the last wave of emigrés to America, so Malik is more disposed to the idea of emigrating, too.

Two beers

Two beers.
The four-hour-early end of shift
when enough work's been done
and all that's left is
to chew the words of the day
and spit tomorrow's words,
like drops of ambergris,
into the ocean of the evening.
Between long drinks,
Leigh blows *shisha* smoke
towards the makeshift roof beams:
double-apple or apple-mint,
the invocation of some burned
dessert from childhood.
Two beers.
ABF expats drag plastic chairs
near the oscillating fan
that blasts a manic cool
across mismatched tables.
The self-appointed elite-in-exile,
they wear an indifferent face
and sip cheap white wine
from clunky tumblers.
We order dips and Persian bread,
and discuss our team;
their antiquated attitudes,
little hope and tired minds.
Two beers.
Nima comes to turn the coals
and breathe fresh life
into Leigh's expiring pipe.

Another bread to scrape
the dips' last stains
from the unfired bowls
and we laugh at on-shore's
latest diktat to be ignored:
'A symposium of clowns –'
'– except for Sam –'
'– except for Sam.'
The swinging fan blows away
the *shisha* smoke and our small laughter.
Two beers.
The night has settled soft now;
the ABF have gone
and only the fan whispers
judgement on the sudden
empty space.
Exploding foliage reveals
three rats chasing unseen shadows
along the fence and up onto
the roof beams above our heads.
They scan the patio below
for food scraps and the
stalking danger of Nima's cat.
Two beers.
The Nauru darkness squats
like vengeance over the Island Café.
Locals drink in other bars
where cheaper beers are served
by Chinese women whose men
smoke Winfields through rotten teeth
and whisky breath.
Refugees don't drink.

They do the work that no one wants,
to build a nest of rocks
among the dry stones
of savage barren living
through endless savage barren days.
Two beers.
Midnight and the rats have gone,
the *shisha* stands extinguished
on the table
beside the empty bottles
and unused ashtray.
Tomorrow, it will start again:
the twelve-hour shifts
cut short, the rats and locals,
the *shisha* smoke and Nima's food.
But tomorrow someone else
will drink the beers while we
fly out for three weeks' life at home.

Nima, his wife, Katy, and their eight-year-old daughter live in and run the Café Island (known to the expats as the Island Café). The food is unpretentious Persian cuisine, the beers whatever Nima can source from Capelle's supermarket on the other side of the island. The building is ramshackle, the café toilet is the family bathroom, the outside patio has been built entirely by Nima out of timber and other materials he has been able to find by scavenging. Rats live in the shrubbery along the perimeter of the café and chase each other along the beams and rafters of the roof, and Nima's cat is half their size. Nima and Katy are hard-working, decent, friendly and intelligent. Their business is successful and would be even more so if it were situated in Sydney or Melbourne.

In Protest

Lip-sewn against vocal protest, women crowd
the fence in rigid vigil over their own
long dying.
Eyes alone scream above stitched and muted mouths
as, unheard, their silence is ignored. Unseen, the proud
defiance of their death is carved in stone-
faced lying.
The pride, the silence and the eyes: one last way out.

Local guards, fearful and dull, look on.
Unsure what to do, they do nothing. They stare
in bovine
incomprehension, like children at a death.
One whispers, laughs; impossible rapprochement
between two cultures paralleled to infinity, where
the long line
of inequality shadows life's uneven breath.

Somewhere in the camp, an emasculated
father self-immolates while his sick child
lies dengue-weak and fevered in its bed.

We hear the details later, in unrelated
snippets once the reports are filed:
numbers under observation, numbers in isolation; 'just one dead'.

Naurumour #3

Towards the end of August 2017, Nasratullah's housemate was beaten up by a group of Nauruans, outside his own house in the settlement of Nibok, and his smartphone was stolen.

Nasratullah and his housemate are both refugees and are both employed by the Australian company contracted to run the centres, and all attached activities, on behalf, and under the aegis, of the Australian Border Force (ABF). They are both respected in their workplace and are patient in their dealings with authority, a patience learned over many years of displacement from their families, and over the four years they've spent under the sometime brutality of detention.

The assault and theft of the smartphone were reported to the Nauruan police immediately after the event and the police, as is usual, and therefore, as has come to be expected from the local police, did nothing. They listened to the account of the assault and they listened to the account of the theft without taking notes and without taking an interest. This is not an uncommon situation: gangs of locals, many young, many less so, on occasion get drunk and roam the likely roads and tracks used by refugees coming home from, or going to, work. The locals attack the refugees, often beat them with weapons and steal their possessions: phones, motorbikes, small change, whatever the refugees are carrying at the time. Nothing ever happens from a legal perspective when the perpetrators are Nauruan and the victims, refugees.

Anyway, Nasratullah's housemate, having reported the incident to the correct authorities, and having received no meaningful response, approached the ABF to report it to them.

The ABF predictably replied, 'Go to the police.'

When the ABF were told that the incident had already been reported to the police but that nothing had been done about it, they washed their hands of it as it was 'a police matter'.

The end.

Except that this is not the end: if and when the Manus Island refugees are transferred to Nauru, the balance of perceived power will shift. The Manus refugees are all single male, all vying for alpha status on Manus, and have all proved to be intolerant of what they see as the poor treatment of refugees, or bad behaviour by the authorities. More than eight hundred seriously disenchanted men arriving on Nauru will see the Nauruan police force stretched beyond their capability (which is minimal at best) when they have to contend with and contain riots and rioters. The Manus Island refugees will not tolerate corrupt indifference to their grievances. (December 2017)

Mehdi's song

Born into a foreign land, he
lives a cuckoo life among
smaller and much drabber birds.
He wears dull feathers and learns their call
to pass unnoticed through the Deobandi
Mutaween who throng
the city in blackheart backwards
persecution of those who fall
outside the narrow confines
of some arbitrary mullah's creed.

Aged fourteen, Mehdi walks his daily path to school.
He sees the thug squad at the iron gate
and fears some dire transgression of an arcane rule,
but also sees his fear has come to him too late.

The crows begin to circle. In search
of carrion they scour the city
for the unknowing dead and dying,
for misfit supplicant emigrés
who drag with broken wing to church,
who crawl in hope – at least – of pity
in place of wanton hate. Corvid crying
sets deep harsh misery over days
that string unending, in tangled lines
towards no future, with undue speed.

So Mehdi, now fifteen, flies north
over borders undefined in the shade
of strangers who, for money, venture forth
into terror lands where colours fade.

Language none and custom less
and broken nights in constant shift,
followed fast by empty days in hiding
from the eyes the shadows the traitorous tongues
that, for a bowl of watery dhal, will confess
the cuckoo's whereabouts to the state: his life, a gift
from one whose own life is also riding
the same unsure treacherous wind. Young
fledgling birds, unnested far from home,
seek only to stay one beat ahead.

At sixteen, Mehdi has flown the lethal city
and crossed the mountains and the desert
for the coast. Ahead, a night-time granite sea
before Australia; freedom in the land preferred.

Weeks in boats and trucks and desperate
houses. Caged in foodless Bogor rooms with heat.
Crammed with others and their diseases, little
water, sanitation. The cuckoo bird is back
among the dull and damaged, though now
the dull and damaged are also separate
from the drabber birds as they beat
their cuckoo wings in lame and brittle
protest against their past, a cul-de-sac
of memories to remind them how
life, fear-leached to toneless monochrome
existence, flutters one last wingbeat away from dead.

Mehdi spends his birthday on the unruly ocean.
Seventeen and headed, finally, to Australia.
Seventeen and sunk by the water's wild commotion
in a stunned non-swimmer's drowning bacchanalia…

Seventeen and rescued in a mid-sea drama
that leaves him staked on Christmas Island,
where others flock in tumult, lost in their own trauma;
just another solitary cuckoo bird in the hand.

Ten months later and he hears his fate:
he'll move with twenty others to Nauru –
a word…and alien sound…a made-up destination…

His eighteenth birthday and the date
is lost somewhere in the slew
of forty bodies bivouacked in frustration.

Nineteen…twenty…twenty-one and the dates
are lost among the stinking slew
of forty bodies bivouacked in degradation.

and then another year…another two…
and still the forty bodies and no salvation.

Mehdi looks on death; his one chance, his only chance
of relocation.

Three scenes

i.

A thirty-year-old refugee works at the supermarket next to the bank. He is one of the anonymous thousand or so refugees who patiently wait to be processed and transferred to the US as part of the Obama deal. He has few possessions, few demands and few expectations now that the deal belongs to Trump.

One of his possessions is the small motorbike he uses to get to and from work. It seems that everyone has a motorbike on Nauru: refugees, locals, women, men, youths. Sometimes an entire family can be seen riding a 90cc bike along the road that circles the approximately twenty-five kilometres of coastline around the island. Sometimes, when fuel is scarce – which it often is, because of the erratic supply to the petrol stations – large Nauruans on these machines can be seen leaning into the windows of friends' cars and coasting along in neutral to save fuel. Motorbikes are everywhere. They are ridden on the road, on the footpaths, on the rough ground of open private and public spaces. Whenever one is behind the wheel of a car, one remains constantly aware of the dangers posed by helmet-less bike riders.

So, the refugee supermarket worker finished his shift, went to the gym for a couple of hours, and headed home on his small motorbike. The speed limit on Nauru's main road is fifty kilometres an hour and almost everyone abides by this law: refugees more than anyone, because refugees are a soft target for the local police, and the local police are not averse to harassing refugees for fun or profit. His route took him past the airport and past the Menen Hotel, up the hill, over the brow and down the other side, towards the harbour. Near to the harbour is the building complex known as 'the village'. The village, until November 2017, was where Wilson Security staff and ABF staff lived, while other expats were accommodated either in RPC1 or, in the case of management, the Menen Hotel.

As the supermarket worker – let's call him Abdul – as Abdul was passing the harbour, pootling along under the speed limit, a car approached from the other direction. There's no reason to believe that the car was travelling faster than the speed limit, as no witnesses have suggested this to be the case. However, what is agreed upon by everyone who watched the course of events, is that the car indicated that it was turning off the road; that is, it was turning left. (On Nauru, as in Australia, vehicles drive on the left-hand side of the road.) Abdul was aware of the car. As he was about to pass it in the opposite direction, the car, still indicating left, turned right directly across his path.

Abdul broke the windscreen of the car with his head.

He spent three days in the RON hospital (primitive care at best) suffering a head wound, pain in his ribs and difficulty in breathing.

The occupants of the car were three ABF personnel and one IHMS (International Health and Medical Services) staff member. Witnesses claim that all four of the car's occupants were drunk.

During his three-day stay in the hospital, Abdul received no visitors from ABF or IHMS or from his case worker with the company responsible for the welfare of all refugees and asylum seekers on Nauru.

No police action was taken.

Abdul's injuries continue and he can no longer fulfil his duties at the supermarket, so he has lost his job.

ii.

An Iranian left his country three months before his wife. This is a common occurrence with those fleeing persecution, as it's often the men in these societies who face the most danger. He ended up on Christmas Island. His wife, when she followed his exit for safety reasons of her own, also washed up on Christmas Island.

Happy reunion. Until the husband was relocated to Melbourne in Australia, while his wife was transferred to Nauru a short while later.

She has now lived in the Anibare district for four years with no possibility of being reunited with her husband because Australia's policy is for no 'illegal immigrants' or 'boat people' or 'those transported by people smugglers' to be allowed ever to set foot in Australia, while her husband will find it extremely difficult to travel outside Australia, should his wife ever leave Nauru.

This story is so commonplace that it barely even registers in the consciousness of the uninvolved... We are all involved!

iii.

Two expat teachers were shopping in one of the general stores on the island. These stores sell whatever they can get hold of: car radiators next to nappies, next to cases of Fanta, next to fishing rods. If you can't find what you want in one shop, you try another and another until you can.

For the most part, these shops are converted forty-foot sea containers, windowless and stifling. The owners are invariably Chinese immigrants originally brought to the island to work the phosphate, but who are now the middle-class entrepreneurs of Nauru: 'middle-class' means they are prepared to work – poverty is only a single sale away.

So the teachers were in the shop searching for whatever it was they wanted, one was browsing near the cash till, the other rummaging in the near-darkness at the back.

Suddenly, the one at the back called out, 'Hey! Do you recognise this?' She was holding up a package of Australian-branded, industrial-length toilet paper, the type used in the accommodation blocks in RPC1, the refugees processing centres and the settlement sites where ABF-controlled activities were run. There was a stack of the rolls for sale.

No one questioned for a moment who might have stolen the store of toilet paper and no one ever bothered to report it.

How to get to Nauru #4

Ghazni city lies in Ghazni province a little less than two hundred kilometress south-west of Kabul in Afghanistan. Ghazni province is an area unofficially controlled by the Taliban and elements of al-Qaeda. Information on Ghazni (city and province) is readily available on the internet and it has obviously been a historically significant centre for trade and culture involving many invading nations since the seventh century. It's probably for this, and other, reasons that Ghazni has such an ethnically diverse population. The city stands on a plateau more than two thousand metres above sea level in a region of severe drought and suffers snow-ridden, cold winters and warm, dry summers.

By 2013, Nasrat's family were generational natives of Ghazni and they lived in relative comfort in a city of unreliable commerce where Nasrat's father ran his own fuel supply business with contracts to supply the military and major electricity networks. Comfort, however, doesn't equate with stability or safety in any area of Afghanistan, especially in light of the terrorist organisations' presence. And supplying fuel is always going to prove contentious as it's perceived by all factions not in receipt of the fuel that the 'wrong side' is being supplied.

Nasrat – healthy, bright, untroubled – was fifteen years old and on his way to school on a morning like any other morning when the world as he knew it, ceased to exist. Two men on a motorbike screeched to a halt beside him. The pillion rider leapt from the bike and pointed a gun at the boy, screaming at him to get on the bike with a warning that, should he shout for help, he would be shot. Nasrat complied in shock and fear, wedged between the two men on the back of the bike, as they roared away out of the city. Nasrat is convinced that the men were Taliban and he believed at the time that his life was in danger – to the extent that he thought he would die at the end of the ride.

As they neared the outskirts of the city, they heard gunshots close by and realised – or, at least, the two Taliban members realised – that they were being fired on by a rival faction whose territory they were travelling through. The bike went down in a semi-controlled slide and the men took up positions to return fire at their assailants. Suddenly, the outskirts of the city had become a war zone with gunfire ricocheting down the street.

Try to imagine what Nasrat felt at that precise moment: a boy en route to school, kidnapped and thinking he would die, shot at by unseen gunmen after falling from a speeding motorbike… How would he be expected to react? Freeze in fear…paralysed by shock…? Even in a city of constantly anticipated violence, these events would be traumatic to the most hardened inhabitants. But for a young boy…?

What Nasrat actually did was to seize his chance when his kidnappers were occupied in saving their own necks by leaping to his feet and sprinting back into the city suburbs and, finally, to the safety of home. Home, where his father admitted that he'd just received an aggressive phone call telling him that he had betrayed Islam and that his son had been lucky to escape: next time, the caller asserted, Nasrat would not be kidnapped, he would simply be shot.

For a close and loving family, this threat was incomprehensible: they could never have imagined such a thing. Nasrat was immediately confined to the house, where he stayed for a week without once venturing outside. His mother had the first of her four bouts of severe anxiety or panic attacks, each of which resulted in her being hospitalised. His father decided that Nasrat must be sent to a safer place, even if that meant that the unimaginable became reality: son and parents would be separated for the first time. His father made the heart-wrenching and life-changing arrangements.

The following events have become a little blurred in Nasrat's memory so that the details are sometimes sketchy – sometimes, they're incredibly (and scarily) clear. In 2013, Nasrat drove with his father into Pakistan, where they stopped at a house that had obviously been determined before they'd left home. Nasrat is unsure as to whether this house was in a town or in the countryside, an uncertainty that he attributes to his being confused by trying to process what was happening. What he is sure of, though, is the fact that there were five or six other people in the house and that he was kept there for twenty days. His father had returned to Ghazni.

At the end of the twenty days, Nasrat was taken to an airport, where he boarded a plane to Malaysia. How long was the journey? Which airport did they take off from? He has no idea. He took his seat for the flight and immediately fell asleep because of the exhaustion he experienced as a result of the stress of his 'captivity'. He slept for the entire flight.

Nasrat is unable to say in which city the plane landed, although it's almost certain to have been Kuala Lumpur. He remembers being in the airport for two hours, during which time his and his fellow migrants' passports were taken from them and handed over to a third party: a member of the people smuggling group that was handling the arrangements. Eventually, they were herded out of the airport and into a waiting car, which drove them to a house at an unknown location.

It's important to stress that Nasrat, by the time he reached the age of nineteen, had a strong command of English, was outgoing and sociable with a sharp and well-defined sense of humour that manifested both verbally and in his writing – in a language he hadn't understood a word of four years earlier. When he arrived in Malaysia, and when he was shunted around like inanimate cargo, he was dulled, divorced from what was becoming his new reality, and so unaware that he completely stopped living in the moment. For that reason, he couldn't say how long the car journey from the airport was, which direction they travelled or how many people were in the vehicle. He was, in his own words, 'depressed and sad'.

He stayed in the Malaysian house for twelve days and was forbidden to leave under any circumstances whatsoever. Food was delivered to the house by car and the people – 'guards' – spoke a mixture of Pashto and Urdu, so it seems likely that they were of Pakistani origin. Nasrat, however, was probably in a state of clinical shock during his residence in the crowded house, and was unable to communicate meaningfully with anyone, so he never really knew.

At the end of his near-two-week stay in the house, he was driven through the night to an unknown destination with some of the other migrants. They finally came to a halt, after several vehicle changes, in the jungle while it was still dark, but Nasrat knew that they were near a beach because he could hear the lapping of waves not too far away. They walked a short distance before coming to the shoreline that he'd known was there and they had to wade out into the ocean to reach a speedboat idling off the shore. This added another layer of trauma to Nasrat's already fraught constitution: he was unable to swim and had a consequent fear of water. Forcing himself to overcome his fears, however, he made it to the boat and settled himself on board for the four-hour trip to Indonesia, where they beached near an isolated house, again in jungle. Inside the house, a woman mimed to the migrants that they should stay quiet and low, the implication being that the consequences would be dire should they fail to comply.

By this time, Nasrat was sick with, among other symptoms, vertigo. This was probably brought on by lack of adequate food, poor sleep, constant fear and a general disorientation due to the haphazard movement he'd been subjected to. Health matters such as those, however, were of little or no importance compared to survival in a clearly hostile world, and Nasrat suffered stoically and, to a great extent, silently.

Because of his sickness, he remains unsure as to how long he stayed in the jungle house, but he recalls being transported to another airport by car, where he took a plane to Jakarta. Meeting him at Jakarta airport was yet another agent of the people-smuggling team in a car with tinted windows that was driven through the streets until they came to the Sabnoz Hotel in central Jakarta. The hotel is commonly used by people smugglers to house refugees as it is close to the UNHCR (United Nations High Commission for Refugees), where asylum seekers can be processed to determine their true refugee status. Nasrat stayed in the

Sabnoz for three nights and he says the hotel was 'overcrowded with people in transit'.

Following a well-worn transit route for those like himself, Nasrat was next taken by car to Bogor, two hours from Jakarta, where he was kept locked up in a house for more than six weeks (he can't remember if he was holed up for forty-five or forty-seven days) before being driven, again by car, for two hours to a rendezvous with a convoy of trucks. There were three covered trucks, each of which held more than thirty migrants, that drove non-stop for sixteen hours to a large beachside villa. The migrants were given only a little bread and water during the sixteen-hour drive through near-unbearable heat.

Once they'd reached the beachside villa, they were made to hide quietly during the day so as to not attract attention to themselves. Again, Nasrat is unsure how long he was at this particular house as he was, again, sick. The occupants of the house were soon taken, five or six at a time, in a small boat out to a bigger boat moored offshore. This vessel had a covered upper deck, a lower cabin and a capacity of thirty, including crew. Approximately one hundred and five migrants were loaded onto the boat. As Nasrat was unable to swim, his fears increased on the overcrowded boat and again he feared for his life.

The boat set off in choppy seas and seasickness quickly became a problem for the majority of the passengers. Already sick, Nasrat's condition worsened the more he became dehydrated from vomiting over the side of the boat. They spent three nights aboard the craft before the navigation system broke down and they were left drifting without steering. The seas became rougher and the waves threw the boat around like a toy. Most of the migrants aboard the vessel gave up all hope of survival until an Australian navy vessel appeared to rescue them.

They were taken to Christmas Island.

Nasrat's account of the next six months is a carbon copy of all the other accounts by unaccompanied children: he couldn't walk on land for a full week because of his seasickness, he shared accommodation with other minors, segregated from the adults on the island, he was given little or no information about what would happen to him. Until he was told he had five minutes to pack his belongings as he was going to Nauru – unsurprisingly, a place he'd never heard of.

The flight to Nauru was almost as traumatic as the boat trip that landed him on Christmas Island: there were more police or immigration officers on the flight than asylum seekers, surveillance cameras monitored everything the passengers did (which wasn't much, as there was one officer – Nasrat thinks they were police although they might have been Immigration or ABF – assigned to each asylum seeker), they were forbidden to undo their seat belts unless they needed to use the toilet (which had to remain unlocked and open for observation). And they were not allowed to wear shoes.

On arrival in Nauru, Nasrat's story is, again, the same as everyone else's story, with only observational variations. For instance, he was terrified by the slum housing he saw when driving from the airport to the processing centres (this slum housing is the standard residential housing of the locals) and, when he first saw the white tents he was to be accommodated in, he thought he'd arrived at 'our cemetery'.

After four years on Nauru, Nasrat has been given his visa for the US as part of the second wave of refugees to leave under the Obama deal. He still suffers health problems, with intermittent fever, vertigo and recurring colds.

Nauru Refugee Blues #2

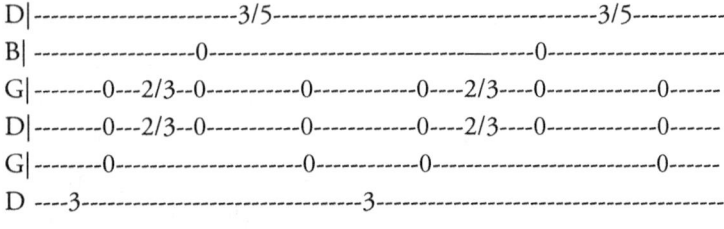

I got a notice this mornin', how do you reckon it read?
It said, ten more years on Nauru till your life is dead.
Yeah, got an RSD this mornin', I say how do you think it read?
You know, it said, ten more years on Nauru, man, until your life is dead.

So, I left my wife and children, and took off down the road.
I went to see the doctor 'fore I'm layin' on a coolin' board.
I left my wife and family, and I said I took off down the road.
Said I'm goin' to see the doctor, babe, 'fore I'm layin' on a coolin' board.

Well, the doctor he done told me, said you've come to the wrong place.
Said, there's nothing wrong with you that can't be fixed on Judgement Day.
Yeah, the doctor he done told me I come lookin' in the wrong place.
Ain't nothing he can do to help till along the Judgment Day.

Looked like there was a thousand people waitin' sad-eyed standin' round.
I didn't know so many was waitin' to be laid down.
Looked like a thousand were just waitin', sad-eyed standin' round.
You know, I never knew so many were waitin' to be laid down.

I said to the doctor, said, 'Please have mercy on my soul.
I can't stay here no longer, not for all your weight in gold'.
I said to the doctor, 'Sir, please have mercy on my soul.
You know I can't survive here no more, not for twice your weight in gold.'

Well, I folded up my arms and I slowly walked away.
I said, 'If there's nothing you can do for me, I'll see you on Judgement Day.'
Ah, yeah, I folded both my arms and alone I walked away.
I said, 'I guess I'll see you later then, on the comin' Judgement Day.'

You know Nauru ain't no place to live, so I knelt right down to pray.
The Nauru blues came by and drove my prayers away.
Yeah, this island ain't no place to be, I said I kneeled on down to pray.
But the Nauru blues came right on by and drove my prayers away.

You know Nauru ain't no place to live, so I fell down on my knees.
The dark night Nauru blues came by and they just swallowed me.
I said, this island ain't no place to die, yeah, I fell on down on my knees.
But the Nauru blues came right on by and they just swallowed me.

Yeah, Nauru ain't no place to live, it's earth's last place to choose.
Break your aching heart and soul, the Nauru refugee blues.
I say, Nauru ain't no place to die, it ain't the place I choose.
It breaks my aching heart and soul, the Nauru refugee blues.

The evening before I fly out

I watch you standing on the beach at night,
the moon – a spinning coin, a hanging peach –
suspended like holographic hope, out of reach,
elusive behind its sun-reflected light.

You move on patient feet towards a pitch-black sea
whose surreptitious waves dash forward with a hiss
to whisper harsh unwanted truths in the ellipsis
of perpetual retreats that, despondent, sigh between
the rippled forays frothing on the sand.
The water has more depth than all the mystery
of the world, each drop the unplumbed history
of all things – yet the water quickly dries on your hand.

The moon – a little fuller – will be here again tomorrow,
the whispers of the sea will never leave this shore.
And you? Will you continue to stare out across the more
or less infinite ocean? The hologram of hope, I think, is hollow.

The last few cents are spent on hope renewed.
The untasted fruit, invisibly wormed and rotten,
dies on the tree within the sound of death. Most often
like the remorseless echoed pounding of solitude.

Amicus Nick Martin *sed magis amica veritas*

When, finally, even doctors speak out
there must be a problem.

The oathen illuminati, wrapped
masonic in coats of allegiance,
constrained by hard-constructed caskets
of confidentiality, are bound
to maintain a silence
to protect the vulnerable
in their care.
Yet one (or two) stand up
and occupy a higher ground
that offers greater protection.
One (or two) proclaim a truth
in the face of righteous ignorance
or of barefaced wilful duplicity
and lies.

When those on the ground, festooned
in laurelled plaudits,
provide incontestable front-line evidence
of failure
(negligent or systemic or, in the
guise of democratic policy – deliberate,
cynical and inhumane)
we know there must be failure.

Four thousand two hundred
and eighty kilometres:
the distance between truth
and lies,
the distance between failure
and culpability.
The distance between those
people corralled in the narrowing
tunnel of despair
and self-harm,
and the smug and pompous
puff-balls bent on pandering
only to their own self-generated power.

Also caught,
the one (or two) who favour
'first, do no harm'
but then
'do good',
the one (or two) who, with words,
reveal inaction,
who reveal malign intent,
who reveal base cynicism,
who reveal, ultimately,
national shame.
Nostra culpa.

The final few

The final few – how do they feel?
Small beneath a bone-shard moon abandoned
to the limitless backdrop of infinity,
a moon that hangs like the last thought before a sleep
that might never end? The Obama deal
is done and all the other refugees are gone,
flown to freedom from such base captivity
as is found amongst the jagged phosphate rocks and deep-
fissured pinnacles and wind-stunted poisoned trees:
a butterfly tempest island, plagued by flies.

So, do you think they ever wanted a life forever haunted by lies and isolation?
Do you think they ever thought a fugitive from mass slaughter
would find only prejudice and privation?

Paired for solace or shared reason
(or else in damaged mistrust they live alone).
The ancestral wisp-cloud moon spills silver light
on the broken dark-stained stones of memoried towns
where generations, easy bound in blood-and-breath cohesion,
built brick on sweat-stained brick, bone on bone,
while some cruel and fearful Mammon acolyte
burned the map and pulled all history down.
Vermilion fades to rust and then to these
dun dirtshades mirrored in blind eyes.

So, do you think they ever wanted a life forever haunted by lies and isolation?
Do you think they ever thought a fugitive from mass slaughter
would find only prejudice and privation?

Time is all there is, and time unspools
unseen as now and now repeat forever
in the present. Moment follows moment
as an instant replication without past
or future: the wider world, with all attendant rules,
spins in a different space to bring together
a more conventional view in which each component
of linear time is linked and then held fast
in straight connection to the law of threes:
what was, now is, then will be, with all that that implies.

The final few – how do they feel?
Chronosynclastic days all merge as one.
The lunar illusion fails to hide the truth
that it hangs unchanged from night to darker night.
Only the 'what if' and its searing mental pain are real,
and only nightime offers sad relief from a revealing sun
that illuminates the scars and warts of rotting youth.
The final few – hiding in the shadows found on a midnight
island, all sense of time and place and self, all sense of ease
destroyed. The final few, alone, forgotten. Traumatised.

So, do you think they ever wanted a life forever haunted by lies and isolation?
Do you think they ever thought a fugitive from mass slaughter
would find only prejudice and privation?

Resignation Letter

Dear Xxxx,

I am writing to officially tender my resignation from Xxxxx Xxxxx (Xxxxx) (current service provider) as Education Team Leader on Nauru…

While I have greatly appreciated my time on Nauru, working in the welfare space, the stance taken by Xxxxx Xxxxx (current service provider) management towards additional work time for our locally based employees (LBEs), and refugee staff in particular, is in my opinion morally insupportable.

I have voiced my concern at management level that our LBEs should be receiving ten hours of training per week, which is paid as additional hours, to bring their total working week up to fifty hours. I am disappointed that Xxxxx (current service provider) is resistant to allowing these hours, as I know that it makes a significant difference to the daily lives of the refugees who work under extremely difficult conditions on the island.

(…)

The mental health, well-being and supported upskilling of the team can also be greatly enhanced by the investment of 10 additional hours – specifically for training purposes (…), which to date has been an area in need of considerable improvement by Xxxxx (current service provider). I feel strongly that if employing LBEs to do meaningful and important work can help them maintain good mental health, then it is a great investment compared to the costs associated with providing mental health services to those very same people.

I note with disappointment that at management level I have heard phrases such as 'we need to turn them (LBEs) into professionals', and 'they (LBEs) need to be ready for the real world', as arguments for not allowing additional hours for LBEs, when in fact offering quality training will do just that. I have also been told we should have 'professional standards and expectations' in relation to LBEs which is certainly true; however, I feel that this must be a two-way street, and meeting professional expectations in this area is something that Xxxxx (current service provider) has not done well to date.

(…)

While leaving the company on good terms, and in a professional manner, I would like to make it very clear to the board of directors that I think things are not at all equitable in the welfare space. The refugees who work for Xxxxx (current service provider) are, first and foremost, our clients, and secondly, they are our employees. When management uses fiscal arguments in situations such as this, it is not appropriate as the situation is more complex than mere small sums of money. We have a duty of care to the refugees who work for us that is more far-reaching than the usual employee/employer relationship, and therefore should also influence the way that decisions are made in relation to the provision of support and services.

LBEs have been instrumental in helping Xxxxx (current service provider) maintain service delivery during difficult times of expat staff shortages and represent an extremely reliable and cost-effective source of staffing which makes the provision of ten additional hours a win-win situation because we can keep an entire workforce feeling valued and looked after at minimal expense when compared to the costs associated with expat staff; it just makes good business sense.

(…)

Management has made the argument that 'they (LBEs) signed up for this', and 'they (LBEs) can leave at any time', which to me are clear indicators of a lack of sensitivity, an inherent arrogance, moral turpitude and an inadequate understanding of the difficulties faced by refugees living and working for Xxxxx (current service provider) on Nauru. The LBEs whom I know are proud to work for Xxxxx (current service provider), and the language used by management and all Xxxxx (current service provider) staff should show respect for the pride LBEs continue to show in their work and for their company.

I would have liked to have continued in my position, but I am choosing to resign after more than two years here, as the attitude towards LBEs that has been communicated and demonstrated to me by management is not consistent with my morals, and what I consider to be good business sense, and a fair go for all.

I would like to remind you of the message in today's pre-start notices: 'Knowing what's right doesn't mean much unless you do what's right.'

I hope that my resignation can bring light to this issue, and that you give it your careful consideration for future planning of the company's direction, as Xxxx (current service provider's) treatment of LBEs will greatly affect its reputation in the region and its ability to secure future major contracts in the welfare space.

Yours sincerely

Xxxxx Xxxxx

Email from a refugee granted a visa to the States

Good afternoon to you all

As most of you know, today is the last day of my work and I wanted to take the chance and send my gratitude to you all as I count myself the luckiest person who got to meet you. During my job with Xxxxx (former service provider) and Xxxxx (current service provider), I got the chance to meet you all which turned to be the best thing ever. Each one of you taught me a lot of things that I would have not learnt anywhere in the world. I would like to thank you all for the nonstop support that helped me get through rough times here in Nauru. You will always be remembered as having you in my life will always remain special.

If there is any grammar errors, just ignore it as I am not good at expressing my feelings through writing.

Make sure to be in contact through my personal email.

With all the love and respect

    Nasrat

This email was sent to the team in which Nasrat worked for exactly one year as an Education Assistant: essentially, a trainee teacher of English language. Four years ago, when he arrived on Nauru, he spoke no English at all. He was, at the time of writing his email, twenty years old.

www.ingramcontent.com/pod-product-compliance
Lightning Source LLC
Chambersburg PA
CBHW071119030426
42336CB00013BA/2148